Reflections and prayers

Copyright © 2010 Margaret Hopkinson
All rights reserved. No part of this book may be reproduced or transmitted in any form or by any means, electronic, mechanical, photocopying, recording or otherwise, without the prior written permission of Margaret Hopkinson and Morse-Brown Publishing.

Published by Morse-Brown Publishing
506F The Big Peg, 120 Vyse Street, Hockley
Birmingham B18 6NE
Photography © Margaret and Graham Hopkinson
Design & Production: Morse-Brown Design Limited.
↗ www.morsebrowndesign.co.uk

ISBN: 978-1-907615-01-6

INTRODUCTION

These reflections and prayers have been written over many years. Most of the reflections were inspired by the wonders of God's creation. The prayers came to be written because I realised that the psalms were a wonderful prayer resource, but I often struggled with the language of the psalmist. So I decided to capture the main thrust of the psalm in my own words, and then I found that I could use them in my praying again and again.

Much later it occurred to me that the reflections and psalms might go well together, each reflection leading into a response of praise and worship or a cry for help; and here is the result.

Interspersed with the reflections and the accompanying psalms there are photographs and additional praise psalms. There is an introductory "I Come" psalm which can be used for coming into God's presence and the final reflection stands on its own without an accompanying psalm.

The photographs have all been taken by my husband Graham and myself, and mostly come from our holidays together and there is an index at the back which indicates where each photograph was taken.

My thanks go to Graham without whose encouragement and help this book of reflections and prayers would not have been written.

I COME

Lord God as I come into your presence today,
I call out to you for mercy.
I thank you that you don't keep a record
of my sin and failure, but instead,
you give me
the gifts of forgiveness and restoration.

....

I come to you in childlike trust;
like a fretful child who is calmed
in the loving arms of her mother,
so I rest in your unfailing love.

....

I come to wait for you;
as a traveller who enters a dark tunnel
longs to see the glimmer of light at the end,
so I wait for the light of your presence and truth.

....

I come and wait... and as I wait,
I put my trust and hope in you.

Psalms 130 & 131

BEAUTY FOR ASHES
a reflection from Tenerife

Explosion, fire,
searing heat, molten rock,
and the island was born rising out of the boiling sea.
A barren dry arid place –
a heap of cinders,
a pile of ashes,
and yet as I look I see amazing beauty
growing out of this desert land.
Flaming poinsettias,
pure white lilies,
roses in abundance.
The grey stone walls covered with purple and red bougainvillea,
palm trees, cacti,
and dark green conifers on the mountain side.

I thought again of God's promise to give beauty for ashes.
What life and colour has come from this one time ash heap.
A reminder that God is constantly creating and recreating;
the desert blossoms,
winter gives way to spring
and death bursts forth in resurrection life.

HOLY AND MIGHTY GOD

Let us come to the Lord our God
with worship and praise,
for he is a holy and mighty God.

He gives us a sight of his majesty and strength
in the awesome power of nature:
the explosive roar of thunder,
the searing flashes of lightning streaking across the sky,
the force of the wind whipping the sea into a frenzy,
and the devastation of flood, earthquake
and erupting volcano.

Sometimes when we are quiet and still in his presence,
we catch a glimpse of his holiness
and of his mind and purposes,
that are way beyond our human understanding,
and we bow before him lost in worship and praise.

Lord, I remember
that you are the sovereign all powerful and holy God,
but also that you are mindful
of the needs of your people,
giving us both strength and peace
and I come to you today
with my heart full of thanksgiving and praise.

Psalm 29

THE WONDERS OF CREATION

Lord God,
when I look at the wonders of your creation,
the early morning sun glinting on the October tree,
the steady rain of bronze gold leaves carpeting the earth;
when I gaze at the perfection of the crimson rose,
or enjoy the delicate scent of early summer flowers;
when I stand at the edge of the ocean in the face of the wind,
watching the huge waves crashing on the rocky shore,
I see just something of your power and majesty.

I marvel and wonder
at your involvement with men and women.
You have made us in your image,
you have given us responsibility for this world of yours
and you have showered your favour upon us.

O Lord, how great is your name,
you are worthy of all praise and worship.

Psalm 8

CARN INGLI

This morning the mountain was in cloud,
then as the weather began to clear
there were just thin wisps of mist over the top.
Gradually the sun won the battle over the cloud and mist,
and now the mountain is bathed in glorious sunshine.

A picture Father God of your forgiveness.
But do I really feel that I can stand before you
in the brilliance of your presence,
in the comforting warmth of your love,
stand tall and unabashed, hiding nothing?
Do I really know that you have swept away
my offences like a cloud,
my sins like the morning mist?
Or do I still feel unclean?
I don't find it so difficult to believe
that you forgive my specific sinful acts.
But that I can come cleansed into your presence
when I know there is so much more purifying
to be done in my life,
that I find much more difficult to accept.

The cloud will cover the mountain again;
tomorrow it may be shrouded in mist once more,
but the sun will rise in its strength and power
and banish both cloud and mist.
Tomorrow I will need to come back
for your forgiveness, for your cleansing,
because I know I will fall short of your standards
again and again.

But I come to accept this morning, as I sit in the sunshine,
as I stand in the warmth and purity of your light,
my sins have been forgiven, my offences have been swept away.

CALL TO PRAISE

I will praise the Lord
from the depths of my being.

I will remember his goodness to me,
and give thanks to him.
He forgives my sin, he heals my body,
he gifts me with his love and understanding,
he satisfies me with good things
and my life is renewed and refreshed.

I will praise and give thanks to the Lord
for he has made himself known to me.
He doesn't treat me according to my deserts,
he looks on me with compassion.
His forgiveness is total and complete,
for he wipes the slate clean.

He is a loving Father
who understands my weakness and frailty.
He remembers that my days on earth are short,
but his love for me is not limited by the boundaries of time;
it is so great that it cannot be measured.

Praise him all you heavenly beings.
Praise him all you peoples of the earth.
Praise him all of creation.
Praise the Lord.

Psalm 103

THE GOODNESS OF GOD

I looked out of my window at the snowy scene,
a grey white world,
cold and damp.
The earth lying dormant,
lifeless and desolate.
A sudden movement caught my eye,
a bird flitting from branch to branch,
then another,
and another.
Great tits, blue tits, sparrows and finches,
each tiny creature throbbing with life,
protected and cared for by the goodness of God.
Life in the midst of death.

"Look at the birds of the air" Jesus said.
Lord I look
and see that you created the tits, the finches and the sparrows,
that you sustain their life in the cold of this winter's day.
Then I remember that you also said,
"You are far more valuable than the birds of the air."
Help me to remember the tits, the finches and the sparrows,
when my world becomes cold and desolate.
Help me to know that you will sustain my life
with your tender love and care.

A STRONG TOWER

When my life is in turmoil,
and problems assail me,
when my thoughts chase round and round in my head,
like the relentless turning of a wheel in a mill,
when there doesn't seem to be any way out of my dilemma,
then I cry out to you O God, in my desperation.

I remember that you are a God of love,
that you love me intimately and personally.
I remember that you are all powerful
and a God of action.
You are a firm rock for my feet,
the foundation of my life.
You are a strong tower where I can run for safety.
As a mother bird spreads her wings
to protect her young,
so I can shelter in your loving care.

Lord God,
when my life is in turmoil,
when problems assail me,
I will put my trust in you because you are faithful.

My hope,
my peace of mind,
my rest come from you alone.

Psalms 61 & 62

GOD SPEAKS

The morning and evening skies
tell of your glory and majesty, Creator God.
The rising sun edges the clouds with ribbons of fire
and sets the autumn trees ablaze.
The setting sun sinks behind the mountain peaks,
painting the heavens a translucent blue
turning the clouds into balls of fire.

The wonders of your creation tell us of who you are;
and the words you have spoken
show us how to live in harmony with you.
Your directions and ordinances,
your wisdom and your truth,
are vital for the lives of your people.
They give us light along the way
and show us how to live.
They are as pure as gold
and in following them there is great joy.

But how can I stand before you Creator God?
Show me where I fall short of your standards
and grant me your forgiveness where I fail.
Keep me from open sin that can so easily grip my life.
Guard my mouth from damaging words
and purify my thoughts and the attitudes of my heart.

O Lord God you are my Saviour and my Security.

Psalm 19

MY FOOT IS SLIPPING

One day as I was reading in the psalms I came across some lines that came alive for me in a new and personal way. The psalmist described how he felt that his life was falling apart, "his foot was slipping," he was full of fear and "anxiety was great within him."

This was how I felt sometimes, as though I was slipping, losing my grip and hold on life, anxious thoughts welling up from within. How I needed to know the supporting love of the Lord and the lightness of joy instead of the weight of worry.

A few days later another verse from the psalms caught my eye. This time the psalmist was feeling "bold and stout-hearted" he knew that the Lord had answered his cry for help.

Can you do that for me, Lord? If I call out to you when confidence disappears and the uncertainties of life overwhelm me, will you strengthen and uphold me?

I waited, my question hanging in the air, and the answer came back in the words of yet another psalm.
                    "My God is my rock"

GOD MY ROCK

Lord God, you are my rock,
the solid and sure foundation for my life.

Sometimes I gaze at the high mountains,
so massive and strong;
then my eyes fall to the valleys below
and I see that the streams and rivers
are constantly on the move.
The trees and flowers blossom and flourish,
but quickly fade and die.
The clouds come down like a blanket, then lift again,
but the mountains remain solid and firm.

Lord God, you are my rock,
unchanging in a changing world,
solid ground on which I can place my feet.

You give me strength for the journey,
you protect me from the powers of evil,
you give me signposts to mark out the way.
When the going gets tough
you put out your hand to save me from falling,
you watch every step that I take.

You are faithful and true, you never change;
your love is assured for day after day,
your promises stand the test of time.

Lord God, when everything around me is changing,
when the boundaries of my life are shifting,
when I have no safe place in which to hide,
you are my rock, my security,
the true foundation for my life.

Psalm 18 v1-3, 30-36, 46

INHERITANCE

One day Jesus told a story about two sons and their father.
Towards the end of the tale the father said to the eldest son,
"Everything I have is yours, all I possess I want to share with you."
It was all there for his pleasure and enjoyment
and had been there for years,
but somehow his eyes were closed, his senses numbed.
His life was filled with drudgery and hard work,
he had no time to enjoy his father's love or his father's gifts;
the share of the inheritance was his but he had failed to enter in.

Oftentimes I too am like that elder son,
my eyes are dimmed, my senses dulled,
life is filled with work and I am weary in the Father's service.
Then I hear him say, "Everything I have is yours,
leave the work for a while and come away with me.
Everything I have is yours
and I long to share my riches and my treasure.

To share with you the joyful song of the birds,
bleating lambs calling across the field,
the lazy drone of bees in the warm sunshine,
and the gentle lapping of waves on the shore.

To share the springtime pageant of cliff and sea;
the light dancing on the water,
fluffy white clouds sailing across the sky,
banks of thrift on the dry stone wall,
primroses, bluebells, bright yellow gorse
and the red glow from the evening sun
setting the mountain ablaze.

Take time to enjoy my gifts and my love.
Enter into the inheritance that is waiting.
Remember you are always with me
and everything I have is yours."

SHOUT FOR JOY

Shout for joy, the Lord is King.
He is the mighty God who reigns over all the earth.
All of creation gives praise to his name;
the vastness of the heavens,
the depth of the seas,
the hills and valleys, forests and pasture lands,
and every living creature that inhabits the earth.

Sing to the Lord,
for he is active in his world,
making himself known to those who seek him.
He reveals his love and faithfulness to men and women
and all his actions are righteous and just.
He watches over those who trust in him,
shedding light on their path as they walk in his ways.

Let us join with all of creation,
shouting for joy in his presence.
Let us proclaim his saving power
and his mighty strength.

Praise be to the Lord our God.
Praise the Lord.

Psalms 96 – 100

SING TO THE LORD

Let us praise the Lord.
We will sing to him with all the old songs
and the new ones too,
for he is faithful and just in all his ways.

He spoke the word and the world was created;
the dome of the sky,
translucent blue by day
and studded with sparkling stars at night.
He created the oceans
and set their bounds with rocky cliffs and sandy dunes.

The whole world is full of his unquenchable love.
All earthly power and authority derive from him.
His plans and purposes are steadfast and sure
and no one can stand in his way.
He knows the mind and heart of every person
and understands their motives and actions.

This is our great God.
We rejoice in his love,
as he surrounds and protects us day by day
and we put our trust and hope in him.

Psalm 33

AUTUMN

Brilliant colour,
falling leaves,
short lived beauty,
end of summer.
So long to wait for the renewal of spring.

Sadness,
a deep sadness
and regret,
a shrinking from the cold restrictions of winter.

And yet I know that as surely
as autumn leads to winter
and spring follows fast behind,
I must pass through the seasons of my life;
embrace the autumn,
acknowledge the need for winter,
look for the promise of spring
and welcome the joy of summer again.

THE JOURNEY

Lord God there is something deep within me
that cries out for you.
There seems to be a space, a hole in my life,
that only relationship with you can fill.
You are the Almighty God
and yet you have planted this longing,
this desire within me.

I have set out on the journey to find you,
to learn to walk in the light of your presence day by day;
for a day spent with you
is better than a lifetime of independence.

When I go through hard and barren times,
when you seem to be far away,
give me the strength to keep walking on,
until the valley of desolation
becomes a place that is refreshed again
by the waters of your presence.

I thank you that you are the living God,
who protects and strengthens those
who seek to journey through life with you.

Lord my desire is to live in relationship with you
and in you I place my trust.

Psalm 84

CHOSEN
a reflection from Lanzarote

Sitting on the balcony in the early morning sun,
I found a place of sanctuary and an awareness of the presence of God.
As I looked out over a bank of pink and red geraniums,
to the palm trees and the sea beyond,
I was overcome by the immensity of God's plan for the human race
and my heart was touched by a deep sense of awe and wonder.

A few days later, sitting again on the balcony
listening to the gentle sound of the waves rolling on to the shore
and the constant chattering of the birds in the palm trees,
I remembered that God had said,
"I chose you before the foundation of the world, before ever time began."

Chosen for relationship with God,
with Jesus his Son –
the God of history
the God of creation,
the holy God.

Chosen by God
chosen in my mother's womb
chosen in my childhood years
chosen in my youth
chosen in my middle years
and still chosen in old age.

Chosen and anointed to fulfil God's purposes for my life.
Chosen to walk with him
in the coming days whatever they may bring.

KNOWN BY GOD

Lord you know all my actions, when I sit when I get up,
when I go out, when I lie down.
You know all my ways, the direction of my life,
the set of my purpose and will.
You know every word that I will speak before it is formed,
you know my inmost thoughts.
Lord you have searched the depths of my being,
you know me better than I know myself.

How can I grasp or understand
the wonder of your hand upon me.
Wherever I go I cannot be separated from you,
whether I am far from home, or going about my daily life,
whether I am full of joy and rejoicing, or in the depths of despair,
you still hold me fast, you guide my ways.
When light turns to darkness around me
and I feel cut off from you, you are still there,
for the darkness of night and the darkness within me
are as light to you.

You created me,
my personality, my inner being, my physical body.
You watched over me as I grew in my mother's womb.
I praise you because all that you create is good,
and because I am part of your creation.
You knew every detail of my life before ever I was born.
Your thoughts about me O God are countless,
beyond my understanding,
you never cease to have me in your mind.

I lay my life before you.
Search out my lack of trust in you,
search out all that offends you.
Lead me in your way.

Psalm 139

GOD OF MERCY AND LOVE

Praise to you, O God.

You are a God who draws men and women to yourself,
forgiving sin and pouring out your good gifts.

You are a God of power and might.
By your strength
you created the mighty snow-capped mountains
and you control the raging of the ocean waves.
You clothe the earth with beauty,
blessing it with seedtime and harvest.

You are involved in the lives of your people,
constantly working on their behalf.
Sometimes you refine us as silver is refined in fire.
When we are in danger of slipping,
you put out your hand to save us.
When we walk on treacherous paths
you steer us through to a safer place.

Praise to you, O God.
To you I make my sacrifice of praise,
for you are a God of power and might
and a God of mercy and love.

Psalms 65 & 66

CLINGING

The clematis had pushed its way upward between the edge of the balcony and the wooden fencing. There was a single stem creeping along the balcony floor and day by day I looked to see how much it had grown. Soon the tender shoot was stretching out just above the tiles, totally unsupported and looking very fragile. Then as I watched throughout one day, it gradually lifted itself up, reached for the fence and the tendrils secured themselves against the wooden plank.

I marvelled at the ability of the threadlike tendrils to support the plant, at the way they were able to cling to the wood; without them the clematis could not climb.

I realised that just as the clematis needed to cling to the fence I needed to cling to God. Sometimes it would seem that I am like that fragile stem, vulnerable, out on a limb, not knowing which way to turn, then all I can do is to reach out to God.

As the fence was solid and strong for the climbing clematis so my God is a faithful and dependable support for me.

WATER IN THE DESERT

Lord God,
I am in a desert place
and I cry out to you for rescue.
My relationship with you
has dried up and gone stale.
I am weary and thirsty
for the refreshing waters of your Spirit.

And yet because I know
that your love for me is unchanging
and because I have seen you at work in my life
and in the lives of your people
down the years,
I choose to praise and worship you
and to place myself in your hands.

Just as the tendrils of the clematis
cling to the fence to support the plant,
so I will cling to you.
You are my help and protector
and I believe that I will again
be satisfied with the riches of your presence
and the joy of relationship with you.

Psalm 63

THE TREE

Imagine a great tall spreading tree,
a tree that has withstood the winter gales
and the hot summer sun for many long years.
The roots run deep and wide in the fertile soil,
the trunk is strong and sturdy,
and the branches spread in graceful curves.

In spring it is clothed with a mantle of fresh green leaves
but as the days pass the freshness fades.
Summer sun and rain beat upon the leaves,
until gradually they turn to a dullish crispy brown
and take upon themselves a different kind of beauty.
The first frosts of winter loosen their hold upon the branches
and down they fall, covering the earth with a rich brown carpet.

The tree stands stark and bare against the grey winter sky,
stripped of its covering of green and brown.
But now the true shape and beauty of the tree are revealed,
the strength of the trunk,
the curve of the branches,
and the intricate weaving of the twigs.
Branches and twigs that hold a wonderful secret,
buds that are forming,
getting ready for the coming spring.

ROOTED

Lord God how favoured we are
when we walk in your ways
and put our trust and hope in you.

We are like a tree that is planted in well watered soil;
secured and nourished by its roots,
as it grows from acorn, to sapling,
to a great spreading oak.

So our roots go down deep into your love
and we become strong,
living in the knowledge of that love.
Like the tree, as we pass through the seasons of life,
we may be battered by storms,
drought may cause us to lose sight of you,
but our roots hold firm
in the security of your love and faithfulness.

Lord God keep us walking in your ways,
placing our trust and hope in you,
so that our lives bear fruit
and bring honour to your name.

Psalm 1 & Jeremiah 17 v7

THE LORD IS KING

The Lord our God is King.
We kneel before him in reverence and worship;
we lift our voices to proclaim his praise.

The high mountains speak of his strength;
the roar of the sea and the thunder of the waterfall
speak of his power.
He is a holy God who does not tolerate evil.
His ways are beyond our understanding
and his thoughts no one can fathom.
And yet, as a shepherd cares for his sheep,
so he watches over his people.
Every morning his love is as fresh as the new day
and at night we celebrate his faithfulness.

This is our God.
He is our sure foundation,
the rock upon which we stand.
Let us shout for joy in his presence
and come before him with songs of thanksgiving.

The Lord our God is King.

Psalms 92, 93, & 95

TWO GRAINS OF WHEAT

There were two grains of wheat that grew side by side on the head of corn. The spring rain had watered the soil, the roots went deep, and the grains had formed. Now, nurtured by the sun, they had ripened to a golden brown. The soft wind blew through the cornfield and there was a gentle chattering as the heads of wheat swayed in the breeze.

The first grain said "I don't intend to fall to the ground and die. What a waste that would be! I will fly away in the wind and see the world. I want to be free." Suddenly there was a stronger gust of wind and away flew the first grain... and no one ever heard of him again.

The second grain fell to the earth and very soon he was buried beneath the soil. It was dark and cold – how he missed the warmth of the sun. He was pressed down, hemmed in, restricted. Never before had he felt so alone. He seemed to have lost everything he counted dear, his freedom, his purpose, his expectations, his life, his very self.

Then one day in that dark place he noticed a root beginning to grow, then a tender shoot pushing up through the soil. Each day they became stronger, until the root went down and the shoot struggled out into the light.

Later, much later, that tender shoot grew into a strong tall stem, carrying a beautiful head of corn, bearing many grains of wheat.

THE ABSENCE OF GOD

Sometimes, Lord, I feel that you are far away
and I have no sense of your presence in my life.
My heart is as heavy as stone,
negative thoughts spin round in my mind
and I struggle along without purpose or joy.

How long must I wait, O God
for you to shed your light on the pathway of my life,
to make your presence known to me once again?

Then I stop,
and remember all that you have done;
you have adopted me into your family,
you have forgiven my sin and failure,
you have promised your boundless never failing love.

I remember that you are a faithful God
and a God of love and compassion.
I remember your great acts of power down the ages,
rescuing your people again and again.

So I say, Lord God, I will trust you
because you have said that you are always with me.
I will trust you
to restore to me the certainty of your presence
and the joy of relationship with you.

Psalms 13 & 77

KATIE'S CANDLE

Katie gave me a candle for Christmas.
It was round and white and had tiny silver sparkles all over it.
I put it on my shelf and lit the wick;
at first it struggled but as the fire took hold
the flame became straight and tall,
a symbol of light and life.
It burned for several hours,
sometimes faltering in the draught from the window,
but never going out.

Later I looked again; still the wick burned,
but the candle had lost its lovely shape.
It was diminishing,
the wax was melting,
the edges were uneven;
it was no longer a thing of beauty,
but the flame burned as brightly as ever.
Soon I sensed that it was nearing the end of its life.
I watched as the wick was gradually exhausted,
then it fell over into the pool of wax and the flame died.
The life had gone, there was just the shell of the candle left.

I was sad as I looked at the remains of my candle,
but then I remembered that Jesus had said,
"You are the light of the world."
Is this a picture of my life?
I saw how bravely the candle burned right to the end of its days,
and I sensed the challenge that it brought to me.
When my life is diminishing will I just give up
and let the flame splutter out,
or will I continue to be a light bearer
until the wick is totally consumed?

YESTERDAY TODAY TOMORROW

Today, Lord God as I look back over my life's journey
my heart is full of thanksgiving and praise.
I know your protecting hand was upon me
from the moment of my birth.
When I was young and immature
you showed me the path that I should take.
As the storm clouds gathered and my world started to fall apart
you were a rock and refuge to me;
a rock where my feet could find a firm foothold
when everything else was shifting,
a refuge where I could run for cover
when I was battered by pain, resentment and fear.

Lord God you have been a loving and faithful Father to me,
but once again I stand in need of your reassurance,
I need to know that you will listen and that you will understand.
Don't put me on one side now that I am getting old;
my physical powers are beginning to fail,
sometimes my confidence disappears like a puff of smoke,
younger people may see me as finished, of little value.
Lord God, be my refuge, my trust is in you.

I will always have hope because of who you are.
I will declare your love and faithfulness
to those who are just starting out on their journey.
I will tell them that you are a God who saves and rescues,
that you are a God of integrity whose favour lasts for a lifetime,
you are a rock for their feet
and a secure foundation for their lives.
I will tell them that you are my God
and I will praise you to the end of my days.

Psalm 71

SONGS OF THANKSGIVING

Let the praises of God's people
echo around the world from east to west.
Let the praises of God be always in my heart
as I join the ever flowing songs of thanksgiving.

I give thanks to the Lord for all his ways
are marked by love and compassion.

I praise him for he is a powerful God
rescuing his people in their time of need.

I remember that he is a holy God
whose commands and ordinances
are just and true.

And I rejoice in his faithfulness
as he fulfils his promises again and again.

Endless praise and worship are his by right.
Let all of God's people give praise to his name.

Praise to our holy and mighty God.

Psalms 111 & 113

MOUNTAINS

O, the joy to be in the mountains once again,
such a sense of tranquillity and peace,
after the noise and rush of life in the city.

Sometimes walking beside the river
as it tumbles down from the glacier above,
sometimes wandering through sunlit meadows
gazing up at the distant hills.

Then hiking along the high ridge,
a breathtaking sight of the rugged peaks
as far as the eye can see;
sun, shadow and drifting clouds,
the valley and village left far below.

Finding a place to rest on the way,
perched on a rock close by a rushing stream,
drinking in the splendour of the high mountains,
full of wonder and praise to God the Creator.

GOD MY HELPER

Lord I am in need and crying out for help.

As I look to the vastness of the mountain peaks
I remember that you are the creator of all that I see;
you spoke the word
and the heavens and the earth were formed.
Surely you will be my helper.

When I feel that I am losing a grip on my life,
when everything seems to crowd in upon me,
you are there watching over my every step
and you will save me from falling.

When problems and difficulties surround me,
all day long you are right by my side,
and throughout each night
you keep watch as I sleep.

As I go about my everyday life,
as I come in and as I go out,
you protect me from all the powers of evil
that would assail me.
And your protection is not only for today,
but for every day,
for the whole of my life.

Where can I find help?
Surely the Creator God will be my helper.

Psalm 121

THE CALL OF THE COLLARED DOVES

A meditation based on words from the Song of Songs inspired by the collared doves of Lanzarote.

" My lover spoke and said to me,
'Arise, my darling,
my beautiful one, and come with me.
See the winter is past,
the rains are over and gone.
Flowers appear on the earth;
the season of singing has come,
the cooing of doves is heard in our land.' "

Lord, I can hardly believe that you would say these words to me,
but you are my lover.
You love me with an infinite, tender, unchanging love.
I am beautiful in your eyes, you delight in me,
and your invitation is for me to come away with you.

I have left the dull grey days and the cold winter rains behind;
this is the season of singing,
of revelling in the beauty and joy of God's creation.
Flowers are appearing out of the black volcanic soil,
a riot of colour, delighting the eye.
The cooing collared doves are calling to me each day,
reminding me, Creator God, to sing your praises.

I praise you for the wild grandeur of the rolling waves;
for the muted colours of the conical hills,
silhouetted against the brilliant sky;
Lord, you are feeding my soul, my inner being,
with rest, relaxation and peace.

A few days later I again hear your word,
"Arise, and come with me."

Lord I would come with you today.
Where would you take me?
What would you show me?

I gaze at the vastness of the ocean spread out before me.
The sky is dark and the sea is dull,
but as the sun finds a small hole in the clouds –
behold, a dazzling, shimmering pathway, across the grey water.

A picture of the glory of God –
God's presence with us.
A picture of the glory of Jesus –
Jesus' presence with us in time and place.
Jesus glorified in his death –
not a seemingly glory-filled dying,
but unless the seed is buried and dies, it will not produce fruit.

Much later, on a sun-filled day my mind goes back
to the cloudy sky, the dull grey sea
and the sparkling pathway across the water.
How often I miss the sight of your glory,
my eyes are fixed on the heavy clouds and the winter rain
and I lose sight of you.

I must go back to the winter days –
days that will not be marked by the call of the collared doves,
days that may not be sun-filled and glorious.
As I go back Lord, I thank you for this time spent with you,
enjoying the beauty of your creation
and for the glimpse of your glory and presence in your world.
Help me to remember the bright pathway through the sea,
and to keep looking for your presence when my days are dull and grey.

And as I go back I still hear you say,
"Arise and come with me."

PRAISES TO OUR GOD

Praise the Lord.
Praise him in song,
praise him with all his people,
praise him with dancing and music.

Praise him for the wonders of his creation.
Praise him for men and women made in his image.
Praise him for creatures great and small.
Praise him for the splendour of the mountains,
the power of the oceans, the beauty of the earth.
Praise him for the singing lark, rising up into the cloudless sky
and for the early blossom announcing the coming spring.
Praise him at the end of the day, when the sun sinks into the sea,
painting the heavens with glory.

Praise him for his love and compassion,
for he listens to those who call out to him in sincerity and truth,
he lifts the burden from the shoulders of the weary
and rescues those who are sinking into despair.
Praise him for his great acts of power
and for his promises that never fail.
Praise him for his kingdom that is firmly established
and cannot be moved.

Praise him for he is our Creator
and he delights in all that he has made.
Praise the Lord.

Psalms 145 & 148

INDEX

Page

1	Introduction	
2	Photo	Chartwell – Kent
3	I Come	(Psalms 130 & 131)
4	Reflection	Beauty for Ashes
5	Response	Holy & Mighty God (Psalm 29)
6	Photo	Chartwell – Kent
7	Praise Psalm	The Wonders of Creation (Psalm 8)
8	Reflection	Carn Ingli
9	Response	Call to Praise (Psalm 103)
10	Reflection	The Goodness of God
11	Response	A Strong Tower (Psalms 61 & 62)
12	Photo	Bougainvillea – Madeira
13	Praise Psalm	God Speaks (Psalm 19)
14	Reflection	My Foot is Slipping
15	Response	God my Rock (Psalm 18v1-3, 30-36, 46)
16	Reflection	Inheritance
17	Response	Shout for Joy (Psalms 96-100)
18	Photo	Mayrhofen – Austria
19	Praise Psalm	Sing to the Lord (Psalm 33)
20	Reflection	Autumn
21	Response	The Journey (Psalm 84)

22	Reflection	Chosen
23	Response	Known by God (Psalm 139)
24	Photo	Easter Flowers – Devon
25	Praise Psalm	God of Mercy and Love (Psalms 65 & 66)
26	Reflection	Clinging
27	Response	Water in the Desert (Psalm 63)
28	Reflection	The Tree
29	Response	Rooted (Psalm 1 & Jeremiah 17v7)
30	Photo	Krimml Falls – Austria
31	Praise Psalm	The Lord is King (Psalms 92, 93 & 95)
32	Reflection	Two Grains of Wheat
33	Response	The Absence of God (Psalms 13 & 77)
34	Reflection	Katie's Candle
35	Response	Yesterday Today Tomorrow (Psalm 71)
36	Photo	Mimosa – Lanzarote
37	Praise Psalm	Songs of Thanksgiving (Psalms 111 & 113)
38	Reflection	Mountains
39	Response	God My Helper (Psalm 121)
40	Reflection	The Call of the Collared Doves
42	Photo	Stubaital – Austria
43	Praise Psalm	Praises to our God (Psalms 145 & 148)

ABOUT THE AUTHOR

Margaret Hopkinson and her husband Graham, have lived in Birmingham for many years and they have two sons and three adult grandchildren. They have been members of St John's Church Harborne for more than fifty years. During that time Margaret has been actively involved in the pastoral ministry of the church.

Over the years she has increasingly felt the need to get out of the city and into the countryside, spending time in the mountains or by the sea, where she has been nurtured and refreshed by the wonder of God's creation. Her writing began to develop during her times away from the pressures of life and while she was enjoying the beauty all around her. Like her father before her she has a deep appreciation of the poetry of Isaiah and the book of Psalms, and wanting to use the psalms in her prayers she started to explore the possibility of expressing the main theme of some of them in her own words.

This has been a challenging, exciting and enjoyable adventure and her prayer is that the outcome will be a help and encouragement to many, especially as they seek to draw near to God in prayer.